Birmingham Buses
& Recollections 1958

Contents

© David Harvey 2009
Photos: © as credited.

First published in 2009
ISBN 978 1 85794 325 2

Silver Link Publishing Ltd
The Trundle
Ringstead Road
Great Addington
Kettering
Northants NN14 4BW

Tel/Fax: 01536 330588
email: sales@nostalgiacollection.com
Website: www.nostalgiacollection.com
British Library Cataloguing in Publication Data
A catalogue record for this book is available from the British Library.
Printed and bound in Czech Republic

Acknowledgements

If it were not for the many photographers, known and unknown of fifty years ago, this book would have been impossible. Thanks are due to Barry Ware who provided some of the photographs and valuable information as well as the window bills placed in the buses when route changes or additions were about to be made. Thanks are appreciatively given to Steve Calder who helped to date the photographs and who provided a lot of useful facts. Finally, as always thanks to my wife Diana, who has painstakingly edited and proof-read this book.

Introduction

The year 1958 was very bad for football, motor racing, the French, Cyprus, Iraq and debutantes. The Munich air disaster killed 23 people including the cream of Manchester United's Busby Babes; amongst the dead were Roger Byrne, the England captain, Tommy Taylor, England's centre-forward, and the great Duncan Edwards, of whom survivor Bobby Charlton said that he was the greatest footballer he ever saw. During the year four of the best-known motor racing drivers died in their Formula One racing cars. The French Fourth Republic expired and was replaced by the Fifth Republic bringing the war hero General Charles de Gaulle out of retirement. The EOKA riots in Cyprus led to the deaths of many Greek and Turkish Cypriots as well as peace-keeping British soldiers and while the names of Makarios and Grivas might have been forgotten today, in 1958 they made daily headlines as the Cyprus situation deteriorated. In Iraq, the King and the Crown Prince and the Prime Minister were assassinated in Baghdad, an event which turned the country finally from a monarchy to a republic. On the other hand, it was an excellent year for Antarctic exploration, rock 'n' roll and the Campaign for Nuclear Disarmament.

1958 was the fifth year of the New Elizabethan age, a year of Teddy Boys, thick crepe soles and combed-back Elvis Presley-styled hair, and the Austin A40 car, made in Birmingham, became the world's first hatchback, but it was also the last year that debutantes were presented to the Queen. The family Foot was making headlines in 1958: Sir Hugh Foot, the British Governor of Cyprus, was sinking beneath internecine violence, while his brother Michael was leading the CND's challenge to the Government's nuclear policy. At home the big news was the CND's 56-mile march from London to Aldermaston in Berkshire. The times were rapidly changing with the British Empire and Commonwealth Games in Cardiff being the first to use the word "Commonwealth".

The post-war years of austerity and ration books had gone, but photographs of drab street scenes in this year still showed men with trilby hats and gabardine coats and women wearing long frocks. The "Swinging Sixties" were still over the horizon. Heavy manufacturing industry still held sway in the large conurbations, but already a

Frontispiece: The view over Birmingham City Centre and New Street Station in 1958 gives a idea of how Birmingham looked in the last year before post-war redevelopment and regeneration altered it for ever. In the foreground is the Hill Street-Navigation Street junction, with the great wall of the Queens Hotel towering over the station. Chetwyn's gentlemen's outfitters is on the corner of Navigation Street and John Bright Street in the bottom right-hand corner. In the centre, beyond Queen's Drive dividing the old war-damaged LNWR side of the railway station on the left and the Midland Railway side of the station, is the spire of St Martin's-in-the-Bull Ring Church. Waiting at the Navigation Street traffic lights are a Ford Consul MkII 204E and a Vauxhall Cresta PA car. Behind these cars is a BCT Daimler CVG6 from the HOV-registered batch working on the 15 service. About to turn right into John Bright Street is an exposed-radiator Crossley DD42/6 working on a 61 service to Allens Cross Estate. On the right in Hill Street is a new-look-front Daimler CVD6 travelling to its Paradise Street terminus on a 48A service from Kings Heath. *R.S.Carpenter Collection*

number of car and motorcycle manufacturers were beginning to look at their labour-intensive practices. Many of Britain's cities, including Birmingham, were already embarking on major redevelopment, both to modernise and to cater for the increasing numbers of cars. The Conservative Party was swept back into power in October largely due to the idea laid down two years earlier by Prime Minister Harold Macmillan that "You've never had it so good", but only the well off could afford to go on holiday abroad. Car ownership was increasing and Britain's first stretch of motorway, the Preston By-Pass, was opened in December, but as if to compromise the image of a fast car on a motorway, the stars of the previous month's Motor Show at Earl's Court were the latest bubble car models built by Heinkel, Messerschmitt and Trojan.

Birmingham's municipal bus fleet also had an unusual year. The aim of the Transport Department was to "have a presence on every major route" and in 1957 they took over the Midland Red route to the Beeches Estate. The two route take-overs in 1958 were to Great Barr and New Oscott which resulted in the reintroduction of 41 pre-war Daimler COG5s on to the City streets after a two-year interregnum. None of these buses were, strangely enough, allocated to Miller Street garage, which operated these three new services.

While the Corporation was seemingly looking backward by bringing these immaculately turned-out buses back onto the road, they were also looking to the future. 1958 was another year in which BCT tried out another demonstrator, VKV 99, a Daimler CVG6/30 on the Tile Cross service. This was trialled alongside the AEC "Bridgemaster" which had been bought during the previous year. It would be another five years before an order was placed and then, perversely, the contract went to Daimler for an initial batch of 300 rear-engined 'Fleetline' buses!

For Birmingham City Transport 1958 was an interesting year. Buses were still being turned out in immaculate condition and a dented panel meant a hasty return to the garage. The bus fleet was at its maximum size with some 1,788 buses on the strength, which, after London Transport, made BCT the largest bus operator in the country. Car ownership, commercial television and better rates of pay in Birmingham's car industry were all beginning to take their toll on the economics of the bus operation. Service cuts such as those routes running from Station Street occurred during the course of the year but post-war bus withdrawals were still three years away.

David Harvey
Dudley, February 2009

Above: **High Street** The crew of 978 (COX 978) take their city centre break outside the Birmingham Co-operative Society department store in High Street. The bus is working on the long cross-city 29 route and has come from the Kingstanding terminus. In a few minutes the crew will rejoin the bus and travel southwards along Stratford Road to the Highfield Road terminus in Hall Green. The bus is a 1937 Daimler COG5 which had been rebodied in March 1949 with the English Electric H28/24R body built for Manchester Corporation and had formerly been fitted as a new body to bus 842 in January 1942. *R.A.Mills*

goods building while on the waste ground alongside Moor Street is a wonderful array of 1950s British cars including a Ford Consul, a Standard Vanguard and a Hillman Minx. *F.W.York*

Above: **Victoria Square** In September 1958, Daimler COG5 1081, (CVP 181), allocated to Hockley garage, passes the grime-encrusted frontage of the Council House and into Victoria Square. 1081 had returned to service on Thursday 1 May 1958 after being repainted. The result of this overhaul was that the bus positively gleamed and yet the whole effect was rather spoilt by the dull, barely polished radiator. The bus is working on that anonymous destination SPECIAL which covered a multitude of operations most of which involved not carrying passengers. *F.W.York*

Right: **The Bull Ring** The redevelopment of the Bull Ring began in 1958 and the area between High Street and Park Street was cleared within months. Birmingham would never be the same again! Climbing the cobbled hill of the Bull Ring is Metro-Cammell-bodied Daimler CVA6 1489 (GOE 489), which is working on the 29A route. At 75 examples, Birmingham had the second largest number of Daimler CVA6s in the country, only being exceeded by Coventry City Transport. These attractive-looking buses were delivered in 1947 and 1948. In the distance is the Moor Street Station

Above: **Congreve Street** The Park Royal- bodied A.E.C. "Regent" III 0961 RT type 1641 (GOE 641), one of the 15 in the batch, turns out of Congreve Street into Great Charles Street when working on the 1A service to Acocks Green. Behind the bus is the imposing Council House extension which was first occupied in 1912. Despite their idiosyncratic appearance, these were extremely pleasant vehicles on which to ride, although even the regular Acocks Green drivers complained about the variable quality of their air-brakes. The buses spent nearly all their lives working from Acocks Green garage although, with their non-standard staircases and the problem that only the drivers at their home garage had been passed out to drive them, prevented them being used on all-day Outer Circle duties. *F.W.York*

1958 Happenings (1)

January
1. Treaty of Rome founding EU implemented.
3. West Indies Federation created.
4. Sputnik I disintegrates.
20. Sir Edmund Hillary reaches South Pole.
20. First radar speed traps in London.
23. President Jimenez of Venezuela overthrown.
29. BMA links lung cancer to smoking.

February
1. Explorer 1, first US satellite, put into space.
   Egypt and Syria united to form United Arab Republic.
5. Col Gamel Nasser First President of UAR.
6. Munich air crash kills 23 passengers including seven of Manchester United's *Busby Babes*. These players were Roger Byrne, Tommy Taylor, David Pegg, Bill Whelan, Eddie Colman, Mark Jones, Geoff Bent.
21. Duncan Edwards dies from Munich air crash injuries.
27. 35 killed in air crash near Bolton.

March
2. Vivian Fuchs completes first overland crossing of Antarctica.
18. Last presentation of debutantes to H.M.Queen.
24. Elvis Presley becomes US Private 53310761.
26. London's first parking ticket issued.
27. Nikita Khrushchev becomes USSR PM.

April
3. Castro revolutionaries begin attacks on Havana.
4. First CND march from London to Aldermaston.
4. Cheryl Crane stabs and kills Johnny Stompaneto, gangster lover of actress Lana Turner.
17. Brussels World Fair opens.
27. de Havilland Comet IV makes maiden flight.
30. *My Fair Lady* opens to rave revues in London starring Rex Harrison, Julie Andrews and Stanley Holloway.

May
3. Aberdeen tram system closes.
9. Pakistan PM Dr Khan Salub assassinated.
13. Riots by French Nationalists in Algiers
18. Lockheed F104 Starfighter sets World air speed record of 1,404 m.p.h.
23. First "flight" of Christopher Cockerill-designed hovercraft..

June
1. General Charles de Gaulle becomes French PM.
9. HM Queen opens Gatwick airport.

Left: **Old Square** On Sunday 12 October 1958, Metro-Cammell-bodied Daimler CVD6 1810 (HOV 810) stands at the 14 terminus in Old Square. 1810 had entered service on 1 August 1948 and was withdrawn on the last day of September 1963 along with 19 others of the class. The bus was working from Lea Hall garage on the 14 group of services during the period when the demonstrators were being trialled. The wooden interior fixtures, moquette seats and tasteful interiors would have contrasted with the new generation of demonstrators being pounded to and from Tile Cross. The CVD6s of this 1756-1843 batch were largely replaced by the introduction of GON-registered Daimler 'Fleetlines' in the autumn of 1963. *D.R.Harvey Collection*

Right: **Victoria Square** A freshly overhauled and positively sparkling 1724 (HOV 724) is working on the 5A service to Perry Common. This batch of 100 buses were the only metal-framed Brush-bodied Leyland "Titan" PD2/1s ever built. 1724 stands on the Colmore Row side of Victoria Square outside the premises of the Blue Star Line steamship line; strangely, next door was the premises of the Canadian Pacific Railway company which also operated ships. The Blue Star Line was owned by William and Edmund Vestey, who formed the Union Cold Storage Company of Liverpool and were grocers and butchers. They commenced operating their own ships in 1909, principally for the carriage of frozen produce initially from South America and China. Services to Australia and New Zealand were inaugurated in 1933. The company was sold to P&O Nedlloyd in 1998, including its name and livery. *R.Marshall*

Below: **Corporation Street** The Erdington bus services were being diverted away from Whittall Street and Steelhouse Lane on Saturday 5 July 1958 and were to travel via Corporation Street, Old Square and Upper Priory. Two of Miller Street garage's stalwarts pass each other on the corner of Corporation Street and Old Square. 2296 (JOJ 296), destined to be one of the last exposed-radiator Crossley DD42/6 to be withdrawn

in September 1967, turns out of Old Square when working on a outbound 65 service to Short Heath. The inbound bus coming from Erdington on the 64 route is a 1954 new-look-front Daimler CVG6 with a Crossley 55-seat body. *D.R.Harvey Collection*

Below right: **Bull Street** On a dark winter's day with an impending storm approaching, one of Liverpool Street garage's hardworking

Daimler CVG6s built in 1949 with Metro-Cammell H30/24R bodies is about to turn into Bull Street from Corporation Street. 1917 (HOV 917), with its saloon lights on, but without side or headlights switched on, entered service on 1 June 1949 and was the last of the class to be delivered until October 1949 when the last 13 were placed in service when Quinton garage opened. Behind the bus, which is working on the 16A service to Hamstead Hill

by way of Handsworth Wood, are the large premises of Montague Burton's gentlemen's outfitter shop which was strategically sited on the corner of Corporation Street and Lower Bull Street *D.R.Harvey Collection*

Right: **Corporation Street** A Brush-bodied Leyland "Titan" PD2/1 Special bus working on the 24 service to Warstock begins to pull away up the hill outside the premises

of W.H.Smith, the newsagent and stationery store. This building, known as Fletcher's Building, was built in 1887 and were the first in Corporation Street to be constructed in brick and terracotta. The driver of 1698 (HOV 698), presumably unaware of this historical nugget, is in charge of the last of Yardley Wood garage's allocation of these elegant vehicles. Drivers of Leylands tended to use their large 9.8-litre 0.600-engined charges somewhat lazily and on pulling away from the Smith's bus stop frequently used second gear resulting in a good deal of juddering from the transmission. *P.Yeomans*

Below: **Snow Hill** 2117 (JOJ 117), one of the quiet and refined concealed-radiator Daimler CVD6s with a Metro-Cammell H30/24R body speeds, down Snow Hill. The bus was one of the last 30 of the class which were allocated to Perry Barr garage. It is working on the cross-city 5A to Court Lane, Perry Common, having started its journey in Portland Road adjacent to the Smethwick boundary. On the right, parked alongside the goods entrance to Snow Hill Station, is a 1956 Hillman Minx Phase VIII which was the final model of this general shape that had been introduced by the Rootes Group in 1949, but the first with an overhead-valve engine. Speeding up Snow Hill towards the distant Colmore Row is a spilt windscreen Bedford CA 12 cwt van. *A.J.Douglas*

The Bull Ring On Wednesday 6 August 1958, just months before the buildings would be demolished as part of the Bull Ring and Inner Ring Road redevelopment scheme, 1835 (HOV 835), a Daimler CVD6 with an M.C.C.W. H30/24R body working on a 58 route from Sheldon, unloads its passengers when almost at its Albert Street terminus. The early-19th-century premises of Oswald Bailey's Army & Navy Stores were on the corner of the Bull Ring and Moor Street. It was a haven for campers and walkers and anyone who required outdoor waterproof work

clothes. Oswald Bailey was taken over by House of Fraser in 1961 but this was long after this once elegant building had been demolished. The shops in Moor Street in 1958 were as odd a collection as could be found in any part of the City Centre! Next to Bailey's was a barber's pole, but this was for a ladies hair stylist. Blake's were surgical rubber goods suppliers, which always caused teenage schoolboys to snigger when they saw the mannequins in their window. Beyond that was an inappropriately named paint merchant called Scraggs, Peter's bookshop and behind the NOT IN USE bus stop were the Misses Kathleen and Nora St John who ran an old-fashioned sweet shop. Finally, in the shadow of the bus was Cantrill's who supplied cork. One is reminded of a "Round the Horne" episode when Kenneth Williams, in a cod-Irish voice, said "Oive had a wonderful toime in Cork and a fantastic toime in rubber!" Ah well, it was a long time ago. *D.R.Harvey Collection*

Below: **Navigation Street** Turning from Navigation Street into Hill Street and about to cross the entrance of New Street Station's Queen's Drive is 2788 (JOJ 788). This Crossley-bodied Daimler CVG6 is leaving the City Centre on the 15 service to Whittington Oval, Yardley. Towering above the bus is the distant 1880s-built, four-storey Guildhall Buildings which occupied the triangular site bounded by Pinfold Street, whose frontages are behind the bus, Navigation Street and Stephenson Street. Parked in Navigation Street is a positive cornucopia of British cars of the 1940s and 1950s including a Morris Minor Series II Traveller, an Austin A40 Cambridge, a Bedford CA van and an Austin A30 van. The only pre-war vehicle is the Ford 7W Ten Tudor, partially obscured by the traffic bollard. *Bristol Vintage Bus Group*

Top right: **Colmore Row** One of the heavyweight new-look-front Crossley-bodied Crossley DD42/6s speeds along Colmore Row in the summer of 1958 when working on the 15B route to Garretts Green Lane. Behind the Crossley is 2088 (JOJ 88), a Daimler CVD6 with a Metro-Cammell body which is on a 13A route to Yardley Wood. 2088 entered service on 1 March 1951 some seven months after the much later numbered Crossley. Behind the Daimler is the impressive Grand Hotel while parked in front of the Crossley, alongside the foreign branch of Barclays Bank, is an early post-war 3622cc Ford V8 Pilot. *S.N.J. White*

Bottom right: **Edmund Street** The Chamberlain Square end of Edmund Street is dominated by Yeoville Thomason's Art Gallery and its "Big Brum" clock of 1885. The Roman-style bridge was completed in 1912 to link the Museum and Art Gallery to the Ashley and Newman-designed Council House extension. Standing in the shadow of the Council House extension bridge, on the wrong side of the road, is 2630 (JOJ 630). This new-look-front Daimler-engined Daimler entered service on 1 July 1951 from Coventry Road garage where it was one of a fleet of 35 new buses introduced to replace the Coventry Road trolleybus services. This bus is waiting in front of 2117 (JOJ 117), one of the earlier 1951-batch of similar Metro-Cammell-bodied buses, which is also working on a cricket special to Edgbaston. *D.R. Harvey Collection*

Bull Street 2585 (JOJ 585) was the first of the short-length Guy "Arab" III Specials fitted with a Metro-Cammell H30/24R body to be withdrawn. This occurred in May 1966 after the bus received severe platform damage causing chassis distortion. In happier times, 2585 pulls out from the bus stop outside the 1926-built Grey's department store in Bull Street. The bus is working on the 31A service to Gospel Lane, Acocks Green. *C.Carter*

Top left: **Albert Street** One of Acocks Green's long-serving stalwarts, 2984, (JOJ 984), waits at the City terminus in Albert Street when parked opposite a 1947 Hillman Minx Phase I. This Guy "Arab" IV with a 55-seat Metro-Cammell body entered service on 1 March 1953 and would survive the take-over by WMPTE by just over two years. These buses had exhaust pipes emerging behind the rear axle which resonated especially in confined spaces and when pulling away uphill. Thus Albert Street was a perfect place to hear these buses roaring up the slope towards High Street. Behind the Guy is an HOV-registered M.C.C.W.-bodied Daimler CVG6 which is working on the 37, a route which had the briefest of destination information stating simply HALL GREEN. *R.Marshall*

Middle Left: **Corporation Street** Seemingly looking the same as the rest of the 1952-batch of Guy "Arab" IVs, 3000 (LOG 300) was the final bus of six which were fitted with constant-mesh gearboxes. It was also the only one of these buses not to have a JOJ registration. Metro-Cammell-bodied 3000 is working on the 55 service to Shard End and is in Corporation Street having unloaded outside Lewis's department store in the distant Old Square. The bus is about to load up outside Roadley's toy and pram retailers and, on the extreme right, Whitworth's cycle shop. *R.Marshall*

Bottom left: **Congreve Street** Only two Daimler CLG5 chassis were ever built and BCT's 3002 (LOG 302), fitted with a lightweight Metro-Cammell body superficially disguised to look like a standard BCT bus, still only weighed 6 tons. Always operated by Acocks Green garage, 3002 loads up in Congreve Street opposite the offices of the Transport Department. The bus, unique among deliveries to Birmingham prior to 1954 with its sliding cab door, is operating on the 1A, a somewhat circuitous route, from Acocks Green via Moseley. *R.Marshall*

Below: **New Street** The appearance of Birmingham's buses was always immaculate as exemplified by 3074 (MOF 74), which is in New Street outside the premises of the *Birmingham Mail*. This Metro-Cammell-bodied Guy "Arab" IV is working on the 3A route from Quinton and is about a third of the way around the City Centre "loop". The bus is about to turn into Corporation Street and is being followed by a Morris-Commercial J-Type van. *S.N.J.White*

Above: **Congreve Street** The first of the 1953-54 batch of Daimler CVG6s with Crossley bodies was 3103 (MOF 103), which was delivered 11 months after vehicles in the same chassis number series. This was because the bus was fitted with a body which had interior fittings made to lightweight specifications reducing the weight of 3103 by ¾ ton to 7 tons 4 cwt compared to the rest of the buses in the class. It was always easily identifiable because of the Auster pull-in front ventilators. *R.Marshall*

Right: **Bradford Street** The 41 pre-war Daimler COG5s which were returned to service between June 1957 and June 1958 tended to be used on either short workings or peak period extras. Dominating the skyline is the tower of the Birmingham abattoir as one of Moseley Road garage's "returnees", 1060 (CVP 160), trundles up the steep hill in Bradford

Street on one such shortworking to Moseley Village. The pre-war bus leads 2578 (JOJ 578), one of the 100 short-length Metro-Cammell Guy "Arab" III Specials delivered in 1950 which is going to Gospel Lane, Acocks Green, on the 32 service. There are no fewer than eight other Corporation buses visible including one coming out of Rea Street on the distant right of Bradford Street. Bradford Street was an old drover's route that led from Camp Hill towards the markets area of the City. *F.W.York*

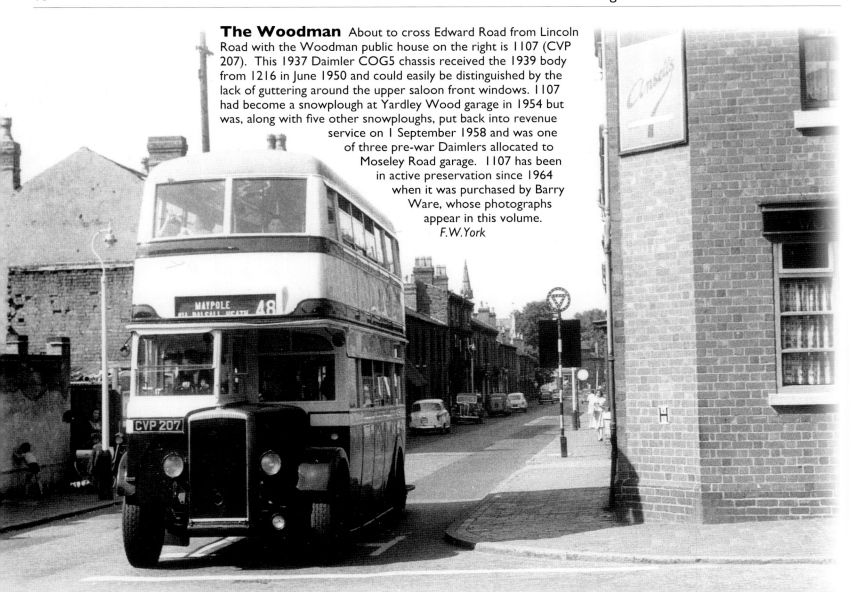

The Woodman About to cross Edward Road from Lincoln Road with the Woodman public house on the right is 1107 (CVP 207). This 1937 Daimler COG5 chassis received the 1939 body from 1216 in June 1950 and could easily be distinguished by the lack of guttering around the upper saloon front windows. 1107 had become a snowplough at Yardley Wood garage in 1954 but was, along with five other snowploughs, put back into revenue service on 1 September 1958 and was one of three pre-war Daimlers allocated to Moseley Road garage. 1107 has been in active preservation since 1964 when it was purchased by Barry Ware, whose photographs appear in this volume.
F.W.York

Below: **Digbeth** The most unusual-looking buses in the post-war fleet were the 15 AEC "Regent" IIIs which had London-style RT type chassis with a very low radiator line. Their Park Royal bodies had a touch of the "horse designed by a committee" look about them, combining all the best features found in Birmingham, London Transport and Park Royal designs, which produced a distinctly unbalanced and frankly odd final product. 1640 (GOE 640) entered service on 5 September 1947 and was withdrawn on 28 February 1963, having spent all its working life being operated by Acocks Green garage. The bus is working on the 44A route to Lincoln Road North and is passing the premises of Smithfield Motors in Digbeth, who were the first sellers of Volkswagen cars in Birmingham. It is also passing an Edinburgh-registered Austin A40 Utilicon estate car dating from November 1955. *J.Cockshott*

Above: **Rea Street, Digbeth** As the Midland Red coach driver walks towards the rear of a BMMO Duple-bodied C1 coach, two Corporation buses pass the entrance to Midland Red's Digbeth Coach Station in Rea Street. Rea Street was an important 200-yard link between Digbeth, the main A41 south-west route out of the City centre to Stratford, Warwick and Coventry, and Bradford Street which served the markets area of the City.

Although both travelling towards Digbeth, the two Corporation buses are in fact travelling in opposite directions. The leading bus is 1897 (HOV 897), a Daimler CVG6 with a Metro-Cammell body, and is travelling out of the City towards Garretts Green Lane on a 15B service. Following it is 2070 (JOJ 70), a year younger new-look-front Daimler CVD6 which is coming into the City towards its terminus in Albert Street on a 50B service from Alcester Lanes End. *M.Hayhoe*

Below: **Digbeth** Harking back to nine years earlier, the driver of 2063 (JOJ 63), pretends to be a tram driver as he lets off his passengers in Digbeth outside the Coach Station while leaving his bus in the middle of the carriageway! This Daimler CVD6 dated from 1 December 1950 and would last beyond 1958 for another eight years until 28 February 1966. These buses, with their easy-change Wilson pre-selector gearboxes combined with Daimler's own extremely quiet CD 6 8.6-litre engine, were extremely refined and well suited the clientele found in Moseley and Kings Heath. The problem was that they were rather thirsty on engine oil and, with their timing chain at the back of the engine, rather difficult to service. *D.R.Harvey Collection*

Above: **High Street, Bordesley** In the autumn of 1958, 2328 (JOJ 328) storms down the gradient on the dual carriageway in High Street, Bordesley. This had only been finished three years before although the planning had been completed in 1939, but were suspended because of the outbreak of the Second World War. This bus was one of Acocks Green's allocation of exposed-radiator Crossley DD42/6s with Crossley H30/24R bodies. This particular bus entered service on New Year's Day 1950 and would remain all its life working from Acocks Green until it was withdrawn slightly earlier than others of the same allocation on the last day of November 1965. 2328 is working on the 44A service from Acocks Green and has just passed the junction with Adderley Street on the other side of the dual carriageway. Adderley Street was used not only by the 19 City Circle route but also by buses accessing Liverpool Street garage. *R.H.G.Simpson*

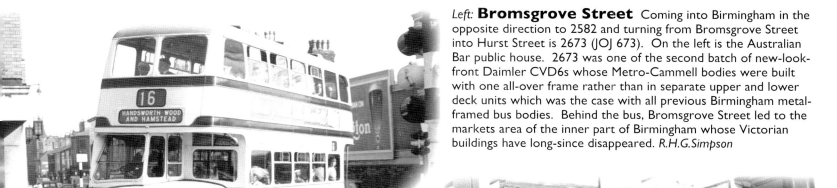

Left: Bromsgrove Street Coming into Birmingham in the opposite direction to 2582 and turning from Bromsgrove Street into Hurst Street is 2673 (JOJ 673). On the left is the Australian Bar public house. 2673 was one of the second batch of new-look-front Daimler CVD6s whose Metro-Cammell bodies were built with one all-over frame rather than in separate upper and lower deck units which was the case with all previous Birmingham metal-framed bus bodies. Behind the bus, Bromsgrove Street led to the markets area of the inner part of Birmingham whose Victorian buildings have long-since disappeared. *R.H.G.Simpson*

Right: **Hurst Street** Travelling out of the City Centre in Hurst Street is one of Acocks Green's buses working on the 32 service to Gospel Lane Loop on the boundary between the municipal housing estate in Acocks Green and Shirley. 2582 (JOJ 582), a 'short' 26-foot-long Guy "Arab" III Special, built to BCT specifications, with a new-look concealed radiator and fitted with a 54-seat Metro-Cammell body, entered service on 1 January 1951 and would have a 21-year career. It will shortly reach the Australian Bar public house and then turn left into Bromsgrove Street. Today this is at the periphery of the Arcadian Centre in the Chinese Quarter of the City Centre. *R.H.G.Simpson*

Main picture: **Melvina Road** The 55 and 56 routes were diverted on 11 August 1957 from the original tramway replacement route along Great Francis Street and Saltley Road to go via Duddeston Mill Road and Melvina Road. 3007 (MOF 7), a Guy "Arab" IV which had entered service in July 1953, is seen in Melvina Road climbing past the railway carriage sidings just north of the then named Vauxhall & Duddeston railway station. (Renamed to just Duddeston in 1974). Here is a line of very early British Railways diesel multiple units including M56168, part of a two-car driving trailer unit built by Park Royal. Towering over the DMU stock are two of the Saltley Gas Works steel framed gas holders. 3007 was allocated to Washwood Heath garage for nearly all of its Birmingham City Transport career. *J.Fozard*

Inset: **St. Luke's Road** A large batch of JOJ-registered 27-foot-long Guy "Arab" IVs were allocated to Selly Oak garage from new. 2951, (JOJ 951), is travelling out of the City in Bristol Street on the 63 service to Rubery. These splendid buses were well suited to the Bristol Road's fast running, though their brakes tended to fade in hot weather on the long hills towards the end of a day's work. As a result the front wings were shortened which lost the symmetry of the 'new-look-front' design, although the wings of 2951 had yet to receive this treatment. By this time the trafficators had been replaced by the first design of indicators which were long amber covers giving a more subtle light than the later flashing units fitted in the mid-1960s. 2951 has just passed St Catherine of Sienna Catholic Church and is approaching the traffic lights at St Luke's Road. *R.H.G.Simpson*

SUBURBIA

Warwick Road, Greet Towards the end of the two-year period after the pre-war Daimler COG5s were returned to service during 1957 and 1958, they increasingly became asthmatic and prone to boiling. As a result they were usually used on short workings and rush-hour peak services. 1027 (CVP 127) is being used on one such duty and is in Warwick Road, Greet, about to cross the Baker Street traffic lights when working on a 44 route shortworking to Stratford Road's junction with Stoney Lane. This bus was one of eight COG5s allocated to Acocks Green garage, but was the only one which had seen service as a snowplough, in this case allocated to Quinton garage until relicenced as a bus on 1 September 1957. *F.W.York*

1958 Happenings (2)

June (continued)
16. Imre Nagy, former Hungarian PM, executed by hanging for treason by USSR-backed Communist authorities.
20. Cyprus curfew after Archbishop Makarios rejects British peace proposals.
20. London bus strike ends after seven weeks.

July
1. St Helens trolleybus system closes.
7. President Eisenhower signs Alaska statehood bill.
10. Earthquake at 7.5 on the Richter scale in Litya Bay, Alaska.
13. 31 killed in violence between Greek and Turkish Cypriots.
14. King Faisal II, Crown Prince Illah and PM assassinated in Baghdad as Monarchy is overthrown in Iraqi Revolution.
18. Prince Philip opens Empire Games in Cardiff.
29. NASA created.

August
4. EOKA chief Col Grivas orders Cyprus ceasefire.
5. Atomic submarine USS Nautilus completes first trip under North Pole
7. Syria seals border with Jordan.
14. 99 killed in KLM Constellation crash over Atlantic west of Ireland.
28. Iceland sets 12-mile fishing limit.
31. Tibetan revolt against Chinese occupation.

September
1. South Lancashire Transport trolleybus system closes.
1. First Cod War between Iceland and UK starts.
2. Dr Hendrik Verwoerd, Afrikaner sociology professor, becomes South African PM.
9. Race riots in Notting Hill Gate.

October
2. EOKA renews violence in Cyprus.
4. New Constitution for French 5th Republic.
21. First women Peers in House of Lords.
28. Cardinal Angelo Roncalli aged 78 elected Pope John XXIII.
31. First heart pacemaker fitted to patient in Stockholm.

November
6. Lord Chancellor ends ban on plays about homosexuality.

December
5. First section of UK motorway opened as the 8-mile Preston By-Pass, later becoming part of the M6.
13. UN rejects motion for Algerian independence.
21. General Charles de Gaulle elected first President of French 5th Republic.
30. Cuban Dictator General Batista about to fall under 23-month campaign by guerrillas led by Fidel Castro.

Kings Heath Travelling along Vicarage Road, Kings Heath, having passed the early post-war prefabs, is 1115 (CVP 215) which dated from 1 November 1937. As per usual for these 41 returned-to-service Daimler COG5s, this bus is working on a shortworking of the Outer Circle route as it returns to its home garage in Wellhead Lane, Perry Barr. Vicarage Road was a strange mixture of different ages of houses with Victorian villas and Edwardian Arts and Crafts residences. Mixed with these were 1920s houses and the aforementioned prefabs which lined the perimeter of the grounds of King Edward VI Camp Hill School for Boys. *F.W.York*

Top right: **Kingstanding Road** 1937 Daimler COG5 1131 (CVP 231) climbs up the steep hill in Kingstanding Road towards the junction with Dyas Road being chased by a Ford Anglia 100E and a Vauxhall Velox. This Perry Barr allocated-bus is operating on the 25 route which was a peak-hours-only service. It will turn right into Hawthorn Road and immediately left into Warren Farm Road before continuing

on to the terminus at Finchley Road. Behind the bus on the opposite side of the dual carriageway is an elevated plot of land which was used for many years as a commercial van sales lot. Just visible is a Fordson E83W, an early 1950s Morris Cowley 10 cwt, a Bedford PC and a much larger Morris-Commercial LC 25 cwt van. *A.Yates*

Above: **Quinton** Speeding along Tennal Lane, Quinton, away from the Quinton Road West terminus of the 10 route, is 1619 (GOE 619). This batch of Metro-Cammell-bodied Daimler

CVG6s could, with the exception of the last four of the class, be distinguished from the later HOV-registered batch by having the front grab rail placed across the upper saloon windows rather than below the windows. In 1958, much of this part of Quinton was still farmland, as exemplified by the distant tractor, or was awaiting new housing development. The sports car special on the left at first sight looks as if it is overtaking the bus, but is in fact just parked on the wrong side of the road! *J.Carroll*

Below: **Vicarage Road** is part of the Outer Ring Road connecting Stirchley to Kings Heath. It is also used by the Outer Circle 11 bus route. Outside the only row of shops in Vicarage Road was the first request bus stop beyond the compulsory stop at Fordhouse Lane's railway bridges. Opposite the March 1957-registered Austin A55 Cambridge car

is the entrance to Kings Road. The bus is working on a shortworking of the 11 route going only as far as Yardley Wood Road as it would then return to Yardley Wood garage where it was their prize possession. 296 (HOJ 396) was one of only two Leyland "Titan" PD2s to be built, originally having the chassis number EX2. The bus entered service in September 1947 and was the first BCT post-war bus to achieve 20 years service. 296 had a Leyland H30/26R body built to the contemporary PD1 body style except for the front cab apron, which left exposed about 6 inches of offside front mudguard. *F.W.York*

Below: **Alum Rock Road** The destination blind on the bus should also read 55B but an old roll has been fitted to 1648 (GOE 648). This bus was one of the ten prototype Crossley DD42/6s and was one of seven of the class to have the Crossley HOE7/4B 8.6-litre crossflow engine. The XOA-registered Ford Thames personnel carrier (they weren't called minibuses in 1958) was barely one month old when the Crossley was parked in Alum Rock Road at the old 8 tram route terminus just short of the Pelham public house which was a 1930s public house located at the Belchers Lane junction. *F.W.York*

Mole Street Parked in Mole Street, one of the back streets of Sparkbrook, is Metro-Cammell-bodied Daimler CVG6 1866 (HOV 866). It is displaying a destination blind for the 36 route, but this is before the route was cut back from Station Street to Sparkbrook. Mole Street was used after 21 September 1958 as the street for

turning round the shortened 36 route. 1866 is facing the wrong way for it to be after the September alterations. Dwarfing the bus and the mid-Victorian terraced housing is St Agatha's Church. This was designed by W.H.Bidlake and was completed in 1901 unusually combining the classic Gothic style overlaid with a heavy emphasis on the Arts and Crafts movement. *F.W.York*

1958 Happenings (3)

OSCAR AWARDS FOR 1958 FILMS

Best Film	Gigi
Best Actor	David Niven (Separate Tables)
Best Actress	Susan Haywood (I Want To Live)
Best Supporting Actor	Burl Ives (The Big Country)
Best Supporting Actress	Wendy Hiller (Separate Tables)

1958 No1 HIT RECORDS

10 January	Great Balls of Fire	Jerry Lee Lewis
24 January	Jailhouse Rock	Elvis Presley
14 February	The Story of My Life	Michael Holliday
28 February	Magic Moments	Perry Como
25 April	Whole Lotta Woman	Marvin Rainwater
16 May	Who's Sorry Now	Connie Francis
27 June	On The Street Where You Live	Vic Damone
4 July	All I Have To Do Is Dream	Everly Brothers
22 August	When	Kalin Twins
22 September	Carolina Moon	Connie Francis
7 November	It's All In The Game	Tommy Edwards
28 November	Hoots Mon	Lord Rockingham's XI
19 December	It's Only Make Believe	Conway Twitty

SPORTING EVENTS OF 1958

March
2. Gary Sobers scores World Record 365 n.o. for West Indies against Pakistan.
25. Sugar Ray Robinson becomes World middleweight champion for fifth time.

April
6. Arnold Palmer wins US Masters golf tournament.

May
3. Bolton Wanderers beat Manchester United 2-0.
18 Archie Scott-Brown killed in Lister at Spa in sports car race.

June
14. First British win in Wightman Tennis Cup for 28 years led by 17-year-old Christine Truman.
16. Tony Brooks wins European GP at Spa in a Vanwall.
28. In World Cup Final, Brazil beat Sweden 5-2.

Above left: **Linden Road** Pulling away up the steep hill from the war-time bus shelter in Linden Road, Bournville, is 2000 (JOC 200). This Daimler CVD6 entered service on 1 November 1949 with its unique JOC-registration and lasted in service with BCT exactly 15 years before serving another 27 months with Wolverhampton Corporation until February 1967. The bus is working on the 26-mile-long Outer Circle 11 route; it has just left the Cadbury Brothers Bournville Village Green and is heading towards Selly Oak. Just visible, coming out of Woodbrooke Road, is one of the 30 Weymann-bodied Leyland "Tiger" PS2/1s which is working on the 27 route between West Heath, Northfield, Bournbrook and Kings Heath. *D.R.Harvey Collection*

Above **Grove Lane** Travelling along Grove Lane towards Oxhill Road is one of the 1949-built all-Leyland "Titans". The bus is working on the 70 route and is travelling alongside the first section of dual carriageway in Birmingham. This was completed immediately before the opening on

20 October 1912 of
the Oxhill Road 26 tram route and,
unlike elsewhere in the City, the trams ran on either
side of the central reservation adjacent to it but not actually on
it. The houses on the western side of Grove Grove Lane, between Philip Victor
Road and the collection of Victorian properties around the public house at the distant Oxhill
Road junction, date from either just before the outbreak of the Great War or just into the Arts and Crafts-
influenced housing of the 1920s. *Birmingham Central Reference Library*

Above: King Edward VI School in Edgbaston Park Road has always had its own bus services and this well-laden Crossley DD42/6 2340 (JOJ 340) will start from the turning semi-circle in front of the school buildings and will join up with the 1A route in Edgbaston Road at the Warwickshire County Cricket ground before going on to Acocks Green. 2340 spent all its life from 1 February 1950 until 31 May 1966 allocated to Acocks Green garage working the 1A, 11, 31A, 32 and 44 routes. The school always

had buses ferrying pupils from all over the City and the well-behaved public school boys must have made for a pleasant tour for the bus crew. *D.R. Harvey Collection*

Below left: **Birmingham Airport**
Parked in front of the original 1939 terminal buildings at Elmdon Airport is 2240 (JOJ 240), a 1950 Leyland "Tiger" PS2/1 bodied by Weymann. Had the order for these 27ft 6in-long 34-seaters been placed slightly earlier, they would have been 30 feet long and seated about 39 passengers, but they were already under construction when the request to alter them was made. The Corporation operated the Airport Special service from Cambridge Street to Elmdon from the early post-war years and on Saturday 12 July 1958 not only is the bus reasonably full but so is the observation balcony on the terminal building, so presumably either a well-known personality was landing at the airport or the plane spotters were watching an unusual aircraft which had arrived at Elmdon. *A.J.Douglas*

Above right: **Aldridge Road** Travelling towards Perry Barr in Aldridge Road is the first of the 7/5B Crossley downdraught-engined Crossley DD42/6s 2396 (JOJ 396). The bus is working on the peak extra 25 service which started at the Finchley Road terminus of the 33 route and, once beyond Birchfield, went into the City Centre following the 29A route through Lozells and Hockley. There were 30 of these synchromesh gearbox buses in

the class and they were the last exposed-radiator buses bought by the City Transport Department. On the opposite side of the road re the premises of Newhall Garages which was the last property before the Birchfield Harriers Alexander Sports Stadium, hidden by the bus. 2396 is being followed by one of Acocks Green Laundry's numerous Morris-Commercial LC5 vans. *F.W.York*

Opposite bottom right: **Coventry Road**
The change driver of the Daimler CVD6 working on the 60 route to Cranes Park, Sheldon, gets into his cab outside Coventry Road garage. 2421 (JOJ 421), one of the downdraught-engined Crossley DD42/6s with a Crossley H30/24R body, has pulled up rather awkwardly in front of the Daimler. On a miserable December day, 2421 is working into the City and is working on the 17 service not long after its extension to Garretts Green Lane when it was also renumbered from the long-standing 15B. In the gap between the buses is a stand in St Andrew's ground of Birmingham City F.C. *D.R.Harvey Collection*

Top right: **Bristol Road** On a snow-covered day in January and being overtaken by a Morris Oxford and a Ford Anglia 100E is Crossley-bodied Crossley DD42/6 2400 (JOJ 400). The bus is working on the 63 service to Rubery and is loading up in Bristol Road near

Priory Road. The Crossleys operated on the Bristol Road routes by Selly Oak garage would at first sight seem less than appropriate for the short headways and fast running required by the timetable on the journeys especially to Rednal and Rubery. Remember that it was only five years earlier that the high-speed 70hp air-brake trams were regularly reaching 40 m.p.h. on the long stretches of reserved track on the old 70 and 71 tram services. The Crossleys had heavy steering, synchromesh gearboxes and Crossley engines which led to a bus which was neither quick off the mark nor particularly fast. Yet they rode like a large private car and had excellent brakes even when fully loaded on the long hills of Bristol Road. Despite these pros and cons, Selly Oak's Crossley fleet managed a creditable 15 years from 1952 when the trams were abandoned until 1965 which was considerably longer than many of the later West Midland's P.T.E. buses achieved on the tough Bristol Road services. *D.R.Harvey Collection*

Left: **Chapel Lane** Waiting in Chapel Lane at the traffic lights at the top of Chapel Lane is an unidentified member of the 2526 class of 100 26-foot-long Guy "Arab" III Specials with M.C.C.W. H30/24R bodies. The bus is waiting alongside the Oak Cinema while behind the bus are the tall factory buildings of the Birmingham Battery. Between the bus and the Plough & Harrow Ansells public house on the right is a 1954 Standard Eight and an Austin A40. The Plough & Harrow public house on the corner of Chapel Lane was built

in the late 19th century when it was known as the New Inn; it was renamed in 1904, just three years after the CBT electric trams were extended from the accumulator tram terminus in Bournbrook to Chapel Lane. *L.Mason*

Below: **Bristol Road** Loading up with passengers on the outbound carriageway of Bristol Road is short-length Guy "Arab" III

Special 2604 (JOJ 604). The bus is at the stop just after Pebble Mill Road. This 54-seat Metro-Cammell-bodied bus is getting rather full as it seems to be getting what drivers called "a three bell load". The need for a police officer to control the queue getting on the bus, especially as it is composed mainly of smartly dressed mothers and daughters, is now lost in the mists of time. On the rear panel of 2604 is the well-known Birmingham advertisement "Avoid The Race For A Car Park Space TAKE A BUS To Any Place". *L.Mason*

This page: **Rocky Lane** On Monday 16 June 1958, the same day that Tony Brooks won the European Grand Prix at Spa in Belgium and the former Hungarian Prime Minister was hanged in Budapest, BCT's

2432 (JOJ 432) waits for the traffic lights to change in Rocky Lane before crossing Aston Road North. The Crossley is being used for driver instruction, or as it was known locally 'a learner bus', and will almost certainly have to wait while the mother, her two girls and her infant in the pram cross the road. Jelf's Crockery Hire Service was located at 105 Aston Road North on the corner of Rocky Lane and was next door to the Graphic Art Service building and a Municipal Bank. *D.R.Harvey Collection*

Below: Heath Way A Daimler CVD6, 2718 (JOJ 718) allocated to Washwood Heath garage when it entered service on 1 September 1951, turns out of Heath Way into Brook Meadow Road. It is working on the 55 route in Shard End's 1950s municipal housing estate. The extension to Heath Way was instigated on 9 December 1951 from the 8 tram replacement 55B bus route terminus at Bucklands End Lane. The Metro-Cammell-bodied bus is being followed by an early post-war Ford Prefect E93A saloon car. *A.Yates*

Below right: Icknield Street was part of the Roman Ryknield Street which ran to the staging post of Letocetum, near Lichfield. In Icknield Street the junction with Hingeston Street was the Atkinson-owned Royal Mint public house. Between 1936 and 1938, the father of the well-known actor Tony Britton was the landlord of the Royal Mint public house. Beyond the public house are the grim rows of mid-19th-century back-to-back houses. This Victorian pub stood, appropriately enough, opposite the Birmingham Mint which was first opened as Heaton's Mint in 1862 and demolished in 2007. Standing at the nearby bus stop on Monday 17 November 1958 is 2797 (JOJ 797), a 1952 Daimler CVG6 with a Crossley H30/25R body which is working on the Inner Circle 8 route. *D.R.Harvey Collection*

Above: **Washwood Heath Road** There is a long row of late-19th-century shops in Washwood Heath Road between St Margaret's Road and Asquith Road. On Thursday 17 July 1958 this thriving shopping centre looked quite busy with a good selection of scooters and mopeds outside Gilbert King's cycle shop. Parked outside the shop is an Austin A40 van while beyond the bus is one of Brooke Bond Tea's famous Trojan 15 cwt vans. The Corporation bus is 2734 (JOJ 734), a Daimler CVD6 with an M.C.C.W. H30/24R body which dated from October 1951. It is working on a 56B service as far as the Fox & Goose which had been the terminus of the Washwood Heath tramcar route. *D.R.Harvey Collection*

Left: **Sutton Coldfield** 3177 (MOF 177), a Crossley-bodied Daimler CVG6 allocated to Hockley garage, had entered service on 1 May 1954. It unloads its passengers at the Banners Gate entrance to Sutton Park while two inspectors check their paperwork and the passengers. The bus is on hire to Midland Red and has a full load of passengers who are about to enjoy the delights of this large park adjacent to Sutton Coldfield's town centre. Following the bus is a large Jaguar Mark VII saloon car which is turning into Banners Gate from Chester Road. *R.F.Mack*

Left: **Henley-in-Arden** On Sunday 14 September 1958, one of Hockley garage's Crossley-bodied Daimler CVG6s is working on hire to Midland Red, presumably when Midland Red were short of available buses. 3175 (MOF 175), freshly repainted and with its tyres painted black for the occasion, is travelling on the A34 Stratford Road at the bottom of Liveridge Hill approaching Henley-in-Arden when on its way to Stratford-upon-Avon. *J.H.Meredith*

Below: **Pershore Road** A 1953 Volkswagen Panelvan travelling along Pershore Road behind the bus is owned by Hawleys, who were bread and cake manufacturers based in Moseley Road. Travelling out of the City is a late 1930s SS Jaguar four-door saloon. The bus working on the 45A shortworking from the British Oak public house in Stirchley's one-way system is one of Cotteridge garage's allocation. 2930 (JOJ 930), a Guy "Arab" IV fitted with a Metro-Cammell body, is passing the rows of large Victorian terraces and villas which lined this section of Pershore Road for about another ten years. *F.W.York*

Top left: **Portland Road** 978 (COX 978) is a 1937 Daimler COG5 which had been rebodied in March 1949 with a 1941 English Electric H28/24R body designed for Manchester Corporation. It is standing at the Bundy Clock in Portland Road on 3 October 1958. Once the driver has 'pegged the clock', the bus will leave this terminus at the Smethwick boundary and go by way of Hagley Road and the centre of Birmingham before going on to Perry Common by way of Summer Lane, Six Ways, Aston and Witton as a 5A service. When travelling in the opposite direction the bus displayed PORTLAND ROAD 7 on its destination blind. *B.W.Ware*

Middle left: **The Uplands** 1009 (CVP 109) was allocated to Hockley garage in September 1957 when it was returned to service. On a misty, raw-looking morning, this Metro-Cammell-bodied Daimler COG5 has found its way to the bus stop outside the Uplands at the 70 terminus in Oxhill Road. Behind the bus is a Park Royal-bodied Leyland "Titan" PD2/1 which would have dated from 1950. Beyond the parked buses, the mobile tea bar appears to be doing a roaring trade with the bus crews. *D.R.Harvey Collection*

Bottom left: **Highgate Road Garage** 1019 (CVP 119) a 1937 Daimler COG5 with a Metro-Cammell H30/24R body, emerges from Highgate Road garage as it goes to Stratford Road to take up service on the 37 route to Hall Green. This bus was returned to service on 1 September 1957 having briefly been Miller Street's snowplough. When the 41 pre-war buses were returned to service, some of them carried advertisements, which in most cases was the first time in their long service lives. Highgate Road garage had only a small, pavement wide area in front of its doors

TERMINI and GARAGES

and it is on this narrow strip that 1879 (HOV 879) is parked. This 1949 Daimler CVG6, being a Highgate Road bus, is changing crews when working on the clockwise Inner Circle 8 route. *J.Fozard*

Above: **Hockley Garage** Standing on the jack with its front axle off the ground as well as having its battery side panels lifted up, 1082 (CVP 182) positively sparkles in the summer sunshine. This 1937 Daimler COG5 is in Hockley garage yard and was one of nine pre-war buses allocated here whose original Birmingham Central Tramways cable tram buildings are on the right. The Corporation tram tracks are still just visible in the foreground leading into the main car sheds which became the bus garage on 2 April 1939. The bus has its destination blind set for the 16A route to Hamstead. *J.Fozard*

which they were originally intended to wear. 1120 eventually acquired this body in February 1949 from 727 (AOP 727), but somewhere in its life lost its nearside front half-drop window which always gave the bus a lopsided, winking appearance. *L.Mason*

services had their termini taken off the local side streets. The bus is a 1939 Daimler COG5 fitted in May 1946 with a new Brush body which was intended to serve as the post-war prototype body. In the event only the 100 Leyland "Titan" PD2/1s received Brush bodies as BCT looked elsewhere for their bus bodies. 1235 was delicensed on 30 April 1955 and only remained out of service until 1 September 1957. It was finally withdrawn on New Year's Eve 1960. *B.W.Ware*

Below: **Northbrook Street** The terminus of the short 95 route was in Northbrook Street and had been introduced on 31 August 1947 as a replacement for the 33 tram. In the distance beyond Lee Bridge and Dudley Road are the gaunt back-to-back three-storey houses in Heath Street. Standing at the Bundy Clock in Northbrook Street is 1134 (CVP 23) whose chassis entered service on 22

Above: **Wellhead Lane Garage** At the end of April 1958, just days before the bus re-entered service, 1120, (CVP 220), an English Electric rebodied Daimler COG5, stands in the forecourt of Wellhead Lane Garage in Perry Barr. The bus has yet to be fitted with destination blinds for the routes operated by Hockley garage. The English Electric body had been built to the streamline specification of Manchester Corporation, but after that municipality's Daimlers were destroyed by enemy action at the company's Radford Works, Birmingham eventually acquired 20 of them. The Birmingham livery really suited these bodies far more than the Art Deco streamlining

Above: **Bearwood** Standing in front of the concrete bus shelter in Bearwood Bus Station on 23 August 1958 are the driver and conductor of 1235 (FOF 235). Bearwood Bus Station was opened in February 1952 when all of the Bearwood bus

November 1937. This bus had acquired a slightly earlier Metro-Cammell body from 978 (COX 978) in February 1949. After being in store 1134 was returned to service on 4 September 1958, just three days before the 42 service to New Oscott was started. It was one of three COG5s allocated to Rosebery Street and was the only one of the three to be a standard COG5, as 814 had a Manchester body and 1235 was the COG5 with the post-war prototype Brush body. *D.R.Harvey Collection*

Below: **Kitts Green** The terminus of the 14E shortworking was used for alternate service buses on the Tile Cross route. In July 1958, in company with the Willowbrook-bodied Daimler CVG6/30 demonstrator VKV 99, 1627 (GOE 627) waits to turn at the Meadway traffic island so that it can go back to the City. This Daimler CVG6 entered service on 1 June 1948 and, along with 1628 to 1630, was first registered for service some four months after the rest of the class. This was due to a delivery mistake

at Metro-Cammell resulting in these four GOE-registered double-deckers having the same body details as the later HOV-registered buses. *S.N.J.White*

Above: **Rednal** A freshly overhauled 1893 (HOV 893), which in 1958 was one of four of the class allocated to Selly Oak garage, turns into the terminus of the Rednal 62 route. The Daimler CVG6 is passing over the abandoned tram tracks, while in the distance is the impressive arc of the wrought iron tram

shelters last used on 5 July 1952. In the background are the trees on Bilberry Hill, one of the Lickey Hills. The Lickeys were an important recreation area donated by the Cadbury family to the City of Birmingham and in the days of the trams, on Bank Holidays and summer Sundays, the Rednal terminus was as busy as any seaside resort – and all for a 5d tram ride. Although in 1958 bus 1893 is loaded to the gunwales, Rednal is only a shadow of its former self. *L.Mason*

Above: **Howard Road** was used by buses working on the Moseley Road shortworking services to Kings Heath. 1940 (HOV 940), one of Moseley Road garage's allocation of M.C.C.W.-bodied Daimler CVD6s, lies over as its crew take their break. The bus is working on the 49 route which replaced the 40 tram route on 1 October 1949. This service went via Leopold Street whose 1 in 13 descent required that all the four-wheeled trams of the 401 class were fitted with oil and air brakes. These brakes failed in the on position thereby preventing runaway accidents. These buses only had triple servo vacuum brakes! *F.W.York*

Right: **Baldwins Lane, Hall Green**
The Drinka Pinta Milka Day advertising slogan was introduced in 1958 and was an immediate success. Compared with contemporary advertisements it was not just the words

of the advert but the style of the lettering which caught the eye. Standing alongside the Bundy Clock outside the Baldwin public house in Baldwins Lane, Hall Green, one autumn evening at 6:05 p.m. is 2001 (JOJ 1), which entered service on 1 December 1949. It would take until July 1953 for the last of the 999 reserved JOJ-registered buses to enter service. *D.R.Harvey Collection*

Right: **Witton** The 39 service to Witton, although one of the shortest in the city, was also one of the most profitable. It had replaced the 3X tram route on 1 January 1950 which had been operated by Witton tram depot, opened in 1882, whose gable end stands against the skyline above the bus. Today it serves as the Aston Manor Transport Museum which is well worth a visit. The newsagent and tobacconist

shop with The Candy Box sweet shop next door and the Witton Square branch of the Birmingham Municipal Bank in the row of 1870s housing were always the only shops on this side of Witton Lane as originally the entrance on the left was part of the Birmingham & Aston steam tram depot. On 28 January 1958 the bus waiting at the terminus of the 39 route is 2103 (JOJ 103), a Daimler CVD6 with a Metro-Cammell body. In the distance, the original Witton Lane stand of Aston Villa F.C. displays an advertisement for the locally made Hercules Cycles. *D.R.Harvey Collection*

Above right: **Oxhill Road** Parked opposite the Uplands public house in Oxhill Road at the setting down stop is 2158, (JOJ 158). This Leyland "Titan" PD2/1 had a Leyland H30/26R body, entered service on 1 May 1949 and spent its entire life at Hockley garage. Here it replaced some of the least serviceable pre-war Leyland "Titan" TD6cs which had in their day replaced the Soho Road trams at the end of March 1939. The actual terminus for the 70 route was about a mile beyond the original tram terminus at the junction with Rookery Road. The Bundy Clock and the pick-up point for the 70 route were in front of the pub. *Photobus*

Right: **The Hawthorns** The cover of the trafficator arm is painted cream which was done intermittently throughout the 1950s by Tyburn Road paintshop although in this case 1958 coincides with the overhaul date of 2176 (JOJ 176). This all-Leyland PD2/1 is about to pick up passengers opposite the Hawthorns football ground, the home of West Bromwich Albion F.C., has the rare distinction of being the highest football ground in England and Wales at 547 feet above sea level. The bus is working on the 72 service which terminated at this point. This was the City boundary with West Bromwich although it was better known

as the Woodman, named after the public house on the opposite side of Holyhead Road. Around the Hawthorns, opposite the football ground, was the large Bradford's Bakery with its wonderful aroma of baking bread. *M.Rooum*

Below: **Court Lane** The 5A route to the 1930s municipal housing estate in the Perry Common area of North Birmingham was extended by about ¾ mile from Enderby Road along the length of Witton Lodge Road to Court Lane. This extension took place on 24 July 1939 making it the last new service to be introduced before the outbreak of the Second World War. A few of the 1,374 council houses on the Perry Common estate are behind the bus. Waiting to return across the City to Portland Road as a 7 is 2497, (JOJ 497), a new-look-front Crossley-bodied Crossley DD42/6. This bus was to remain a Harborne garage bus from its delivery on 1 August 1950 until withdrawal at the end of January 1969. *A. Yates*

1958 Arrivals & Departures

Births

Erica Roe	streaker at a rugby game in 1982	January
Jools Holland	musician	24 January
Miranda Richardson	actress	3 March
Sharon Stone	actress	10 March
Malcolm Marshall	West Indian cricketer	18 April
Andie MacDowell [Rosalie Anderson]	actress	21 April
Daniel Day Lewis	actor	29 April
Toyah Wilcox	singer/actress	18 May
Jennifer Saunders	comedienne	6 July
Christopher Dean	Olympics gold medal skater, 1984	27 July
Kate Bush	singer/songwriter	30 July
Daley Thompson	athlete	30 July
Madonna Ciccone	actress, singer	16 August
Lenny Henry	comedian	20 August
Michael Jackson	singer	28 August
Jamie Lee Curtis	actress	22 November

Deaths

Edna Purviance	silent film actress	b.1895	13 January
Earnest H. Heinkel	aeroplane designer	b.1888	30 January
Christabel Pankhurst	suffragette	b.1880	14 March
Mike Todd	film director	b.1909	22 March
W.C. Handy	jazz musician	b.1873	28 March
Billy Meredith	Welsh footballer	b.1874	19 April
Robert Donat	actor	b.1905	9 June
Douglas Jardine	cricket captain	b.1900	18 June
Alfred Noyes	poet	b.1880	28 June
King Faisal II	King of Iraq	b.1935	14 July
Henri Farman	pioneer aviator	b.1874	18 July
William "Big Bill" Broonzy	blues singer/guitarist	b.1893	15 August
Ralph Vaughan Williams	composer	b.1872	26 August
Marie Stopes	contraception pioneer	b.1880	2 October
Pope Pius XII	religious leader		9 October

Below: **Shard End** As the bus is beginning to fill up with children at the end of the school day, its driver jumps out of the cab of 2356, (JOJ 356) at the Shard End terminus of the 55 route. This manoeuvre was regarded as dangerous and a driver, if seen doing this by an inspector, could be given an official reprimand. This 1950 Crossley-bodied exposed-radiator Crossley DD42/6 was allocated to Washwood Heath garage and is being used on

Below: **Soho Street** The rain pours down, as a woman wearing a Pakamac, strides towards the waiting Corporation bus. Interestingly, despite the weather, the bus is standing at the Bundy Clock and Corporation bus stop rather than at the concrete Midland Red shelter. 2198 (JOJ 198), a Leyland "Titan" PD2/1 with a Park Royal H29/25R body, stands at the City boundary on the bridge over the Stour Valley railway line in Soho Street at the terminus of the B83 route. Until 30 September 1939 this was the terminus of the 31 tram route and the location of Soho Station which was closed on 23 May 1949. *F.W.York*

Below: **Rubery** The Rubery terminus of the 63 route was opened on 6 July 1952 near the corner of Leech Green Lane and the Birmingham boundary. This was considerably

a shortworking to Saltley Road where it will turn round and run back empty to its garage. *A.Yates*

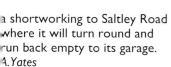

short of the November 1913 terminus where the original bus route, unlike subsequent Rubery tram and bus services, actually crossed the Worcestershire boundary and went into the village to the Rose & Crown public house. When the tram terminus was being constructed at Rubery, a lot of sandstone was excavated from Rednal Hill creating a quarry on the corner of Leach Green Lane. This was to create a large area for a tram turning loop like the earlier one at Rubery; it was never completed, yet it was more than adequate for the replacement buses. Waiting at the outbound Rubery terminus on 16 June 1958 is 2609 (JOJ 609), one of ten of Selly Oak garage's 26-foot-long Metro-Cammell-bodied Guy "Arab" III Specials. It is displaying the ubiquitous Birmingham destination SERVICE EXTRA. *J.Carroll*

Right: **Hawthorn Road** The 28 route started in the City centre backwater of Station Street and proceeded in a south-westerly direction towards Small Heath. Its route then took a parabolic curve around the suburbs and reached its terminus in Dyas Road, Great Barr, which is in the north-west of Birmingham! The bus is unloading in Hawthorn Road not far from the terminus of the 28A route shortworking at Kingstanding Road. 2900 (JOJ 900), was the last of the JOJ-registered Crossley-bodied Daimler CVG6s and along with 2898 and 2899 entered service on 1 July 1953 with the first of the next batch of MOF-registered buses. By 1958, 2900 was allocated to Lea Hall garage which operated the 28 service. *A.Yates*

1958 Happenings (3) continued

SPORTING EVENTS OF 1958

July (continued)
5. Wimbledon: Ashley Cooper beats Neal Fraser for Men's title. Althea Gibson wins against Angela Mortimer for Women's title.
6. Mike Hawthorn wins French GP at Reims in a Ferrari. Luigi Musso killed in same race.

August
3. Peter Collins dies after accident on Lap 11 of German Grand Prix at Nurburgring.
6. Herb Elliott achieves 3 min 54.5 in 1 mile race in Dublin.
24. Stirling Moss wins Portuguese GP in a Vanwall.

September
7. Tony Brooks wins Italian GP at Monza in a Vanwall
21. Peter Whitehead killed in sports car race at Lasalle, France.

October
19. Mike Hawthorn wins Formula 1 title in a Ferrari at final race at Casablanca Moroccan GP, by 1 point from Stirling Moss.
25. Stuart Lewis-Evans dies from burns received in Moroccan GP.

November
10. Donald Campbell sets new world water speed record of 248 m.p.h.

Below: **Sparkbrook** The 36 service was cut back on 21 September 1958 from Station Street to the back streets of Sparkbrook near Stoney Lane, which enabled the bus to go "round the block" and regain its outer route. This was also near to Highgate Road garage which operated the 36 route until the service was transferred to Acocks Green garage when Highgate Road closed on 14 July 1962. 1869 (HOV 869), a Daimler CVG6 with a Metro-Cammell H30/24R body and powered by a Gardner 6LW engine, travels along Stratford Road when working on the original 36 service and is passing the Sparkbrook branch of Lloyds Bank located on the corner of Braithwaite Road. Behind the bus is a rather splendid Austin Sheerline A125 ambulance while travelling on the 29A route from Hall Green is 2145 (JOJ 145), a 1949 all-Leyland "Titan" PD2/1 *F.W.York*

NEW ROUTES and ROUTE CHANGES

Dale End The Fordson Thames 15 cwt van was registered in Coventry in February 1958 and was one of the first of the model to be introduced. It is parked in Dale End as the bus working on the newly introduced 52 route from Beeches Estate has to park away from the kerb in order to unload its passengers. 1516 (GOE 516), a Metro-Cammell-bodied Daimler CVA6, entered service on 1 September 1947 and remained in service for 16 years. *F.W.York*

Station Street The alternative City terminus of the Stratford Road tram routes was located in Station Street alongside New Street Station. Station Street was at one time an important City terminus with services starting from here not only along Stratford Road but also, between 1934 and 1951, the trolleybus routes to Yardley, Sheldon and Lode Lane. The former 18 tram route was replaced on 5 January 1937 by the 46 service to Hall Green. On 16 August 1958 the last bus to operate this service was the freshly repainted 1871 (HOV 871). This Metro-Cammell-bodied 1949-vintage Daimler CVG6 was one of Highgate Road's allocation of these hard-working buses. *B.W.Ware*

Aldridge Road Travelling into the City along Aldridge Road on the newly introduced 42 service is one of Miller Street garage's exposed-radiator Crossley-bodied Crossley DD42/6s. 2303 (JOJ 303) is passing the entrance to Holford Drive where until just three years earlier withdrawn Birmingham buses were stored prior to disposal. Where the Post Office Karrier Bantam lorry is parked formed part of a very wide grassed area that later became the inner section of the dual carriageway road. In the late 1920s the Corporation tramways Department obtained powers to extend the Perry Barr 6 route to Kingstanding and, although these powers were never pursued, a good deal of Aldridge Road and most of Kingstanding road were built with wide central or side reservations for the trams which never came. *F.W.York*

Sheldon Heath Road 5 December 1958 was just two days before the 15B service was extended from the 1949 Sheldon Heath Road terminus to the Meadway and renumbered 17. The huge early 1950s Garretts Green Technical College dominates the Sheldon Heath Road junction with Garretts Green Lane in this large post-war municipal housing development. While an early 1937 Austin Cambridge 10/4 saloon has applied its brakes to descend the hill to the traffic island opposite the Technical College, the bus crew take their break at the terminus with the conductress leaning against the Bundy Clock. 1921 (HOV 921) is a 1949 Daimler CVG6 with an M.C.C.W. H30/24R body. *B.W.Ware*

Culmington Road An interloper from Selly Oak garage, 2348 (JOJ 348), a Crossley-bodied Crossley DD42/6, is working on loan to Cotteridge garage. It is standing at the old Culmington Road terminus in Turves Green shortly before the route was extended to Longbridge Lane on 17 August 1958. Beyond the bus is the house belonging to Hawkesley Farm. Behind it is one of Cotteridge's normal allocation, 2934 (JOJ 934), a Guy "Arab" IV with a 55-seater Metro-Cammell body. This bus was one of a batch delivered new to Cotteridge garage on the abandonment of the 36 tram route on 5 July 1952. The destination blind for the 41 service was confusing as Turves Green was not only the name of the road in which the original terminus was located but was also the name of the area! *R.F.Mack*

Scott Arms The introduction of the Corporation 51 route along Walsall Road as far as the City Boundary occurred on 4 May 1958. This replaced the Midland Red 119 route to the Scott Arms at Great Barr. Standing on the opposite side of Walsall Road on the corner of Newton Road is the impressive Georgian Scott Arms public house. This hostelry dating from about 1800, was demolished in May 1966 and was replaced by a shopping centre and an anonymous new public house. 3026 (MOF 26), a Guy "Arab" IV with a Gardner 6LW 8.4-litre engine and an M.C.C.W. body, waits at the newly installed Bundy Clock on the first day of the Corporation's operation of the 51 service. As with all the acquired bus routes along the Walsall and College Roads, the buses were

always operated by Miller Street garage which strangely enough did not receive any of the 41 pre-war Daimlers which were returned to service between 1957 and 1958. *B.W.Ware*

Beeches Estate On 1 September 1957 the former Midland Red 188 route was replaced by the new 52 Corporation service onto the Beeches Estate. The building of the municipal housing estate was begun in 1934 and built for the First National Housing Trust, but as Midland Red had a presence on Walsall Road with its Great Barr shortworking and Walsall 118 service, the Company claimed rights to the Beeches Estate service. The Corporation used the former Midland Red terminus in Beeches Road at the junction with Hassop Road. The conductor, with his leather satchel and Ultimate ticket machine, stand in front of 3010, (MOF 10), a Metro-Cammell-bodied Guy "Arab" IV. It had entered service on 1 July 1953 in

time to replace the Aston Road trams just four days later. *L.Mason*

Below: **New Oscott** Birmingham's Transport Department could not operate buses outside the City boundary because of the famous agreement made with Midland Red on 4 October 1914. It was only after Perry Barr, originally in the Parish of Handsworth UDC, came into Birmingham in 1928 that Corporation buses crossed the old boundary in the same year as the Kingstanding area got its first bus service. St Mary's College, New Oscott, was designed by one Joseph Potter of Lichfield and was built between 1835 and 1838 in an extravagantly Tudor style of red brick and stone dressings. It is set in lovely manicured grounds which creates a peaceful monastic seclusion and is hidden away from the traffic in College and Chester Roads by a boundary of tall trees. It is alongside these trees and next to the Bundy Clock that 3141 (MOF 141), a Crossley-bodied Daimler CVG6, is parked. *F.W.York*

Below: **Tower Hill** Turning left out of Beeches Road into Walsall Road at Tower Hill is another of Miller Street garage's Crossley-bodied Daimler CVG6s. In 1958 Walsall Road was still a two-way road and its reconstruction into a dual carriageway would not occur for many years. Even so it would not be too long before the Beeches Road junction required traffic lights, especially to assist traffic coming from the City Centre and turning right. 3183 (MOF 183) has no such problems as it turns left into Walsall Road with Eccles's newsagents shop on the corner of Beeches Road. Just visible on the left are the sturdy-looking 1930s council houses which so characterised the Beeches Estate. *A.B.Cross*

Below: **Perry Barr** A Crossley-bodied Daimler CVG6 3158 (MOF 158), which had entered service on 1 December 1953, turns right out of Church Road, Perry Barr, and into Aldridge Road. It has been diverted away from the normal inbound 51 route along Walsall Road from Great Barr. The bus will travel along Aldridge Road passing the Alexander Athletics Stadium and Wellhead Lane where Perry Barr bus garage was located before regaining its normal route at Perry Barr Station in Birchfield Road. Beyond the white-coated policeman on directional duty, through the trees, is the tower of St John the Evangelist whose foundation stone was laid in 1831, while to the right is the edge of Perry Park. *A.B.Cross*

Above: **Walsall Road** Midland Red first operated motorbuses on Walsall Road on Christmas Eve 1913 when the 118 service to Walsall was introduced. The service was taken over by the Corporation on 1 September 1957. Standing alongside the recently "planted" Bundy Clock is Birmingham's last "standard" double-decker bus. 3227 (MOF 227), a Daimler CVG6 with a Crossley H30/25R body, entered service on 1 October 1954 and was a candidate for preservation until it was withdrawn on 30 June 1977 after being involved in an accident. The row of 1930s shops stretched as far as the distant Queslett Road which marked the City boundary. *F.W.York*

Beeches Road In places Beeches Road, despite being part of the 1930s municipal housing area of the Beeches Estate, remained almost like a country lane until the 1960s. It was extremely narrow in places while the descent from the Walsall Road junction at Tower Hill, to its terminus at Hassop Road, was surprisingly steep. 3187 (MOF 187), a 1954-vintage Daimler CVG6 with a Crossley H30/25R body, squeezes passed the 1938 Morris Ten Series III saloon, while following the bus is a Morris-Commercial LC4 canvas tilt lorry. *F.W.York*

EXPERIMENTS AND DEMONSTRATORS

Below: **New Street** After having been involved in a front-end accident, 2799, (JOJ 799) emerged from Tyburn Road Works on 18 April 1958 fitted with a fibre-glass Manchester Corporation style bonnet assembly. This did little to enhance the more refined lines of the BCT-style Crossley body. The bus stands in New Street when working on the recently extended 17 service to Garretts Green Lane and is about to be overtaken by Ford Anglia 100E. *J.Cockshott*

Above right: **Old Square** At first sight 2856 (JOJ 856) looks like any other of the 1952-batch of Crossley-bodied Daimler CVG6s as it stands at the 14 terminus in Old Square. Closer

examination reveals that the bus has had its front wings shortened to ensure better cooling for the front brakes. This cutting back of the front wings would occur much later to most of the concealed new-look buses in the Birmingham fleet. The bus was experimentally fitted with 8-foot-wide axles and wider mudguards. In addition it has extra-wide front axle nut guard rings to ensure that the bus could replicate the width of the genuinely 8-foot-wide buses which were already being trialled before decisions had to be made about replacements required for the early 1960s. 2856 was

frequently used to shadow a normal service bus on the 14 route when it ran without passengers. *D.R.Harvey Collection*

Below: **Tyburn Road Works** Standing in Tyburn Road Works on Friday 12 February 1958 is 2880 (JOJ 880), on the day it was despatched back to Highgate Road garage. This was the first of the two Crossley-bodied Daimler CVG6s to be fitted with the Manchester-style front, which had by this time become the standard for new Daimler CVG6s. The effect of the all-blue bonnet and front might have been less ugly had the addition of cream paint on the bonnet lid been applied in the usual BCT places! *D.R.Harvey Collection*

elow: **Old Square** Between 1955 and *9*60 the Transport Department had on *d*emonstration a total of some 12 buses from *A*.E.C., Daimler, Guy and Leyland in their quest *o*r the next generation of vehicles intended *to* replace all the early post-war stock. In *1*956 they were hired the second Crossley *"*Bridgemaster" to be built. 9 JML was fitted *w*ith an attractive Crossley H41/31R body *a*nd was operated from Lea Hall garage. It *w*as subsequently purchased in August 1957 *a*nd was given the fleet number 3228 on 1 *N*ovember of the same year. In July 1958 it is *w*aiting in Old Square to work the 14E route *to* Kitts Green. *S.N.J. White*

bove right: **Old Square** This was the *b*us which Birmingham perhaps really wanted! *V*KV 99 was 30ft long, 8ft wide, had a seating *c*apacity of 74 and a semi-automatic gearbox. *T*his Daimler CVG6/30 had an open-rear-

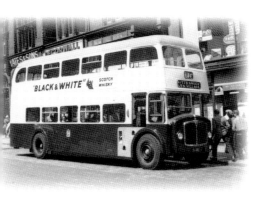

platform Willowbrook body, and was demonstrated to BCT between 23 June and 22 July 1958 and apparently had everything the Corporation wanted. Except… except that looming on the horizon were the next generation of double-deckers and they had engines at the back, platforms with doors at the front, heaters, and were called "Atlantean" or slightly later "Fleetline". VKV 99 is standing at the 14 terminus in Old Square in July 1958 when working on the 14E route to Kitts Green *S.N.J. White*

Right: **St Giles Road** The Tile Cross Estate terminus at the St Giles Road junction with Tile Cross Road was a favourite place in the late 1950s to see the latest demonstrator being tested by the Corporation. The long, low lines of 3228 (9 JML) make an interesting contrast with the then current 30-foot-long Daimler demonstrator VKV 99, which was subsequently returned to the manufacturer and finished its long career in Scotland with McGill of Barrhead. The main problem with VKV 99 was that it was fitted with a Garner 6LW engine of 8.4-litre capacity which made it a little underpowered. *L. Mason*

Index